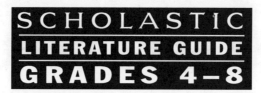

SCHOLASTIC
LITERATURE GUIDE
GRADES 4–8

My Brother Sam Is Dead

by

James Lincoln Collier
and Christopher Collier

Written by Tara McCarthy.
Cover design by Vincent Ceci and Jaime Lucero.
Interior design by Robert Dominguez and Jaime Lucero for Grafica, Inc.
Original cover and interior design by Drew Hires.
Interior illustrations by Eric Angeloch.

Jacket cover from MY BROTHER SAM IS DEAD by James Lincoln Collier and Christopher Collier. Cover illustration copyright © Scholastic Inc. Reprinted by permission of Scholastic Inc.
Author photos on page 4 courtesy of the publisher.

ISBN 0-590-37362-5
Copyright © 1997 by Scholastic Inc.
Printed in the U.S.A.

Table of Contents

Before Reading the Book

SUMMARY

Though set two centuries ago during the American Revolution, *My Brother Sam Is Dead* deals with enduring themes and questions: What's the meaning of loyalty? How are families and friendships affected when their allegiances conflict? How does ordinary, civilian life change when opposing armies overrun the land? For young Tim Meeker, the narrator of the story, these questions boil down to personal ones, such as "Whose side am *I* on: my brother's or my father's? Do I have a part to play in this war? What exactly does it mean to become an adult?" For a while, while the war is fought far away from them, Tim, his parents, and the other residents of the little town of Redding, Connecticut, can delay dealing with many of these questions. But soon Redding is engulfed in the conflict. Tim grows up fast, learning to cope with physical danger and hardship; enduring the deaths of his father, his brother, and his best friend; and taking on the day-to-day responsibilities of an adult.

STORY CHARACTERS

Tim Meeker	Story's narrator
Sam Meeker	Tim's older brother
Life (Eliphalet) and Sarah Meeker	Tim and Sam's parents
Mr. Beach	Anglican minister
Tom Warrups	Last Indian resident in Tim's town
Jerry Sanford	Tim's neighbor and best friend
Betsy Read	15-year-old neighbor; close friend of Sam's
Colonel Read	Betsy's grandfather
Mr. Heron	Wealthy surveyor
Captain Betts, Mr. Rogers, Dr. Hobart, Ned	Dedicated to the Colonials' cause
The Platt family	New York relatives of the Meekers

The Colonial Army chain-of-command

General Wooster	Leader of the Connecticut militia
Colonel Parsons	Sam's commanding officer
General Putnam	Parsons' superior officer
General Benedict Arnold	Chief officer

ABOUT THE AUTHORS

 James and Christopher Collier grew up in a writing family that traces its roots back to Anne Bradstreet, "America's first poet." Their father, Edmund, wrote biographies of historical American heroes such as Annie Oakley and Kit Carson. Christopher Collier mainly followed the historian's path, teaching history in high schools and colleges. James Lincoln Collier concentrated on writing, turning out over twenty books for young readers as well as books and hundreds of articles for adults. In addition to co-writing *My Brother Sam Is Dead*, the brothers have collaborated on several other historical novels for young people. Christopher does all the historical research into true stories of the past. Together, the brothers make up fictional characters for a novel. Then James writes the fictional story within the historical setting.

LITERATURE CONNECTIONS

Other books for young readers set in the period of the American Revolution include (N:nonfiction; F: fiction):

(N) *Can't You Make Them Behave, King George?* by Jean Fritz
(N) *The Secret Soldier: The Story of Deborah Sampson* by Ann McGovern
(N) *Paul Revere's Ride* by Henry Wadsworth Longfellow
(F) *The Fighting Ground* by Avi
(F) *Toliver's Secret* by Esther Wood Brady
(F) *Ben and Me* by Robert Lawson

VOCABULARY

Many of the words below are time-bound, in that they were used frequently in the past but are almost obsolete now (e.g., *breeches*); or are place-bound, in that they refer to a traditional agricultural environment (e.g., *drover*); or have a special meaning within the context of the story (e.g., *cow-boys*, *vanguard*). To help students understand and share these story-words' meanings, assign partners to be Word Sleuths. Word Sleuths define three or four words via story context and via research in dictionaries and historical encyclopedias. Partners (1) write the word's definition as it's used in the story; (2) write an original sentence using the word correctly; (3) write a "distracter sentence" in which the word is used incorrectly; (4) read the two sentences to classmates and ask them to identify the one that uses the word correctly; (5) read the definition aloud.

Chapters 1-5:

ciphering	cholera	leggings	taproom
hundredweight	telling point	prison ship	sloth
loft	Papist	thatch	trainband

Chapters 6-9:

shilling	hardtack	cow-boys	hogshead
breeches	drover	forage	pallet
seining	Johnny cake	woodlots	jerked beef

Chapter 10-Epilogue:

commissary notes	scrip	populace	adjutant
plowshare	vanguard	standard bearer	powder horn
fusillade			

NOTES ABOUT HISTORICAL FICTION

Historical fiction has a setting in a specific, real-life place and time period, and it involves either fictional characters in real-life events, or is a fictionalization of the life of a historical figure. Like other fiction, it has a plot, a conflict, a series of crises, a climax or turning point, and a resolution. Discuss with your students some historical fiction they've already read, such as *Number the Stars*, *Caddie Woodlawn*, *The Drinking Gourd*, or *Journey Home*. Talk about the realities of the settings and how the fictional characters act in believable ways in these settings. Explain that *My Brother Sam Is Dead* is historical fiction set during the American Revolutionary War. Ask: "What do you expect to find out about that war? (*when, where, why, who, etc.*)" "What realistic actions and feelings do you expect of people caught up in a war?" (*e.g., anger, fear, fighting, seeking safety, taking sides*). On poster paper, note students' responses under the heading *Predictions*. Encourage students to refer to the list as they read to determine which of the predictions are affirmed.

GETTING STARTED

You might try the following activities to introduce the book to students. Read aloud the section at the end of the book, "How Much of This Book Is True?". Help the class complete a chart based on these notes. Suggest to students that they refer to the chart now and then as they read the book to see how historical settings and events are woven into a plot involving fictional characters.

My Brother Sam Is Dead

History
Redding, Connecticut, is a real town, and there <u>was</u> a Meeker family.

Fiction
The members of the Meeker family are made up by the writers.

Yale students did rush to join the war.

There was no <u>real</u> Yale student named Sam Meeker.

Focus on the book title, then have students skim through the book to spot some of the many passages in which Sam is very much alive. How does the title "give away" a major event in the story? What big questions does a reader then have as the book begins? (How and why does Sam die?) How do these questions build suspense? Ask students to study the two maps that follow the title page of the book. Discuss why the authors have included the maps, and how readers might use them.

Exploring the Book

CHAPTERS 1 – 5

WHAT HAPPENS

Tim Meeker's brother Sam has left college to join the Revolutionary Army and fight the British. During a brief visit home, Sam and his father (loyal to England) quarrel violently about Sam's decision. Sam steals his father's musket to use as a weapon against British troops, and swears Tim to secrecy. Weeks later, while Sam is lodging secretly nearby, British troops invade the Meeker home and threaten to kill Mr. Meeker if he doesn't give them a gun. Tim rushes to Sam's hiding place and launches a failed attempt to retrieve the musket and take it home. The British soldiers' threat is not carried out; but from his skirmish with Sam, Tim discovers that he himself might be willing to kill to protect his father. Yet, Tim's admiration for his brother's courage endures, and the boy begins to want some glory for himself. When a neighbor, Mr. Heron, asks Tim to carry a secret message to Fairfield, Tim begins to connive a way to do this over his father's objections.

QUESTIONS TO TALK ABOUT

COMPREHENSION AND RECALL

1. Why has Sam left college? (*to join the rebellion against English rule*)

2. What's the big dispute, or issue, between Sam and his father? (*Sam sides with the colonists who want independence from England; his father is loyal to British rule.*)

3. Why does Sam steal his father's musket? (*Sam needs a weapon to use against the British forces.*)

4. Why does Tim try to return the musket to his father? (*Tim's afraid that the British soldiers will kill his dad unless he gives them the family's weapon.*)

5. What does Mr. Heron want Tim to do? (*carry a mysterious letter to Fairfield*)

HIGHER LEVEL THINKING SKILLS

6. The citizens of Redding don't all agree about the colonist-British dispute. What are some of the conflicting ideas among the residents of Redding? (Your students can use the reproducible on page 14 to format their responses. See page 13 for possible answers.)

7. What does Tim admire about his brother? What does he dislike? (*His achievements and escapades at college; his courage in fighting for his beliefs. He dislikes Sam's tendency to argue and fight with his father; his refusal to compromise.*)

8. Point of View: From whose point of view is this story told? (*from Tim's point of view*) Explain to students that this is called the first-person point of view. Ask: In the first-person point of view, whose feelings and thoughts do readers get to know best? (*the narrator's [Tim's]*)

9. External conflict: What conflict in the outside world are the citizens of Redding facing? (*the conflict between opposing armies*) With whom is Tim in conflict? (*his brother, his father*)

PERSONAL RESPONSE

10. Tim's father has a violent temper. How does Tim cope with it? What do *you* think of Tim's way of coping with it?

11. Do you think Tim would really have shot his brother if Sam hadn't managed to get the gun back? Explain.

CROSS-CURRICULAR ACTIVITIES

ART: *Words-to-Pictures*
In Chapter 1 of this story, there are several paragraphs describing in great detail the house—partly-store, partly-tavern, partly-inn—in which the Meekers live. Invite students to use these verbal descriptions to draw a picture or floor-plan of the building. Have students compare their visual renditions and talk about the verbal details they used to construct them. Post the drawings for the class to refer to as subsequent events take place in the rest of the story.

HISTORY: *Schools of the Past*
Ask students to determine from the story some of the subjects that teenagers and college students studied in late 18th-century America. (Examples: "ciphering" [arithmetic]; the Bible; the skill of debating; ancient languages [Greek, Latin]; world geography; history). Have students brainstorm the reasons these subjects were important in Colonial America, which of the subjects are still important to kids today, and what new subjects modern-day students get into, and why.

CIVICS: *The Document That Started the Whole Thing*
Display a copy of the Declaration of Independence, which spells out the ideas underlying many American colonists' reasons for objecting to English rule. As students read *My Brother Sam Is Dead*, take time-out to read, discuss, and have students re-word important phrases from the Declaration and to show how Sam was acting on them. For example, What are *inalienable* rights? In the colonists' (and in Sam's) view, how did the English king violate these rights? What does the Declaration say about ways the colonists tried to resolve these arguments peacefully? According to the Declaration, in what situations are people allowed to "take up arms"?

WHAT HAPPENS

Though it involves lying to his father, Tim agrees to carry Mr. Heron's letter to a man named Burr, in Fairfield. This mission is never completed: Betsy Read, Sam's girl-friend and a Revolutionary sympathizer, wrests the letter from Tim because she thinks it carries information that endangers Sam's life—a surmise which turns out to be false. Weeks later, Tim and his father drive their cattle to the market in Verplancks, New York. Their journey to market is interrupted by cow-boys who try to steal the cattle, but the cow-boys in turn are routed by a Committee of Safety. On the trip back to Redding, how-ever, cow-boys capture and carry off Mr. Meeker, and Tim goes home alone.

QUESTIONS TO TALK ABOUT

COMPREHENSION AND RECALL

1. Why does Betsy struggle to get the message Tim is carrying? (*She thinks it contains information that will put Sam in danger.*)

2. What does the message really say? (*"If this message is received, we will know that the messenger is reliable."*)

3. Why do Tim and his father journey to Verplancks Point? (*They drive their cattle there to sell.*)

4. What calamity happens as Tim and his father head home? (*Mr. Meeker is captured and taken away by cow-boys.*)

HIGHER LEVEL THINKING SKILLS

5. Why does Tim try to avoid Mr. Heron? (*Tim is embarrassed about his failure as a messenger.*)

6. What is Tim's attitude toward lying? (*He thinks it's sinful.*) Why, in spite of his attitude, does Tim begin to lie to his father? (*He wants some glory for himself; he wants to see Sam; he's getting confused about what's right and what's wrong in a setting of war and danger.*)

7. On the journey home, how does Tim avoid capture by the cow-boys? (*He lies: he pretends that he thinks the cow-boys are members of a Committee of Safety that is out to capture these thieves. The cow-boys, alarmed, ride away.*)

LITERARY ELEMENTS

8. Suspense: What uncertainty or anxious feeling do you have as you finish reading Chapter 9? (*What will the cow-boys do to Tim's father?*) Why does this *suspense* make you want to read on? (*to find out what has happened to Mr. Meeker* *and what Tim will do next*) (For more on how the authors create suspense with chapter-endings, use the reproducible on page 15.)

9. Internal conflict: What contrasting ideas and values does Tim struggle with inside his mind? (*Should I be loyal to my parents or to my brother? Should I side with the Revolution or be loyal to King George? Should I always tell the truth, or are there times when it's okay to lie?*)

PERSONAL RESPONSE

10. Have you ever been in a highly dangerous situation? What actions did you take right away? Looking back, do you think these actions were effective? Explain.

11. Mr. Meeker says he doesn't care who—the British or the Revolutionaries—the beef-cattle finally end up with: he simply needs the money to support his family. What do you think of Mr. Meeker's viewpoint?

CROSS-CURRICULAR ACTIVITIES

GEOGRAPHY: *Battlefields of the American Revolution*
Ask a group of students to find—in encyclopedias and history books—the locations of major battles of the American Revolution, and make a large, labeled map to share with classmates. Labels can include the name and date of the battle site and identify which army was victorious or whether the outcome was "undecided."

HISTORY: *Wars on the Home Front*
Like the American Revolution, the Civil War and the war in Vietnam also divided many families and created animosity between neighbors. Encourage students to research these wars using periodicals, books, and the Internet to find out what the conflicting issues were and how people expressed their beliefs through words and actions. To summarize their findings, students can adapt the reproducible on page 14, or write an essay that develops a main idea, such as "War Affects People At Home, Too."

BIOGRAPHY: *Real People in Historical Fiction*
The "Burr" to whom Tim was supposed to carry Mr. Heron's message is Aaron Burr. A general who is referred to often, and who appears briefly in person later in the story is Benedict Arnold. Students can find and read bios of these two Revolutionary War figures, then share with classmates the notorious events (a murder and an act of traitorism) for which they are remembered.

WRITING: *Author Teams*
Read the "About the Authors" section on page 4 of this guide aloud to students. Then have them read the About the Authors section at the end of *My Brother Sam Is Dead*. Discuss how the co-authors cooperated to write a story: one contributed his knowledge of history, the other contributed his skill in constructing an exciting story. Ask student-partners to decide on (1) an historical-fiction short story they'd like to write; (2) how they might cooperate in writing it. Ask partners to firm-up their intended contributions by making an Assignment List. (Partner 1 Will: . . .; Partner 2 Will: . . .)

CHAPTER 10 – EPILOGUE

WHAT HAPPENS

With both his father and his brother gone, Tim takes on the adult responsibility of helping his mother run the farm and tavern and of coping with the demands of rival troops who arrive in Redding. Tim watches in horror as British troops massacre some of his neighbors. He learns that his father and his friend Jerry have died on prison ships. Sam's troop returns briefly to the area. When some of Sam's fellow-soldiers steal the Meeker's cattle, Sam helps Tim recapture them. But as a result, Sam himself is accused of being a cattle-thief. Sam's commanding general decides to execute him to make an example of what happens to soldiers who deprive the army of food. Tim pleads for his brother's life, to no avail, then watches as Sam is killed by a firing squad. In an epilogue written many years after the war, Tim reflects on how he's benefited from the American Revolution, and on the price the dead have paid to secure freedom.

QUESTIONS TO TALK ABOUT

COMPREHENSION AND RECALL

1. Why do the British troops arrest Captain Betts, Mr. Rogers, and Jerry Sanford? (*They are suspected of being sympathizers with the Rebels.*)

2. What awful event does Tim witness at Captain Starr's house? (*the British troops' massacre of the people inside*)

3. Why is Sam allowed to come back to Redding? (*His commanding officer needs Sam's home-town knowledge of Redding.*)

4. What has happened to Tim's father? (*He has died of cholera on a British prison ship.*)

5. Who arrests Sam? (*his fellow Colonial soldiers*). What is he accused of? (*stealing cattle*)

6. What finally happens to Sam? (*He is executed by a colonial firing squad.*)

HIGHER LEVEL THINKING SKILLS

7. Tim says that he "grows up" after his father's disappearance. In what ways does Tim show that he's grown up? (*takes on responsibilities for running the farm and tavern; makes decisions on his own; dares to confront General Putnam to plead for Sam's life; bravely witnesses Sam's execution.*) (Students can use the reproducible on page 16 to show how Tim's character develops.)

8. Tim remembers these words his father often said: "In war the dead pay the debts of the living." How do you think these words apply to Tim? (*Possible responses*: *The dead colonial soldiers have paid with their lives what Tim's family owes for living in a democracy. The dead soldiers have paid the price for their neighbors' inability to settle a conflict peaceably.*)

LITERARY ELEMENTS

9. Irony: Irony is the contrast between what one would *expect* to happen and what *actually* happens. What's *ironic* about Mr. Meeker dying on a British prison ship? (*Mr. Meeker sympathized with the British. You wouldn't expect him to die in the hands of his allies!*) What's *ironic* about Sam's execution? (*Sam was executed by his fellow-soldiers. If Sam had to die, you'd expect that he'd be killed by his enemies.*)

PERSONAL RESPONSE

10. How would you describe Tim's feelings in the Epilogue? Do you think his feelings are natural, or strange? Explain.

11. Suppose you could write a "happy ending" to this story. What would happen in your happy ending? What would the story title be? Would your ending be realistic and historically accurate? Explain.

CROSS-CURRICULAR ACTIVITIES

LOCAL HISTORY: *Conflicts in Your Own Community*
Ask students to explore through community newspapers or local history museums some old or new conflicts that have led citizens to line up against one another. Examples: land use (zoning laws); curfews; school budgets; political campaigns. Students can present the conflict orally and discuss it with classmates: What conflicting ideas are involved in the dispute? Have these conflicts been settled? If so, how?

WRITING: *Your Own "Conflict" Story*
Review with students the first-person point of view as exemplified in *My Brother Sam Is Dead*. Invite students to use this point of view as they write about a conflict they or someone they know has faced. Some students may elect to read their work aloud. To help writers identify and build the strong points in their writing, ask the audience to respond with "I-like-the-part" comments; e.g.: "I like the part where you tell about a conflict between honesty and friendship." "I like the part where you tell what people said as they argued."

ORAL LANGUAGE: *Interviewing Witnesses to War*
Invite students to interview war veterans or people who, as civilians, have suffered through a war on their own home turf. Help students phrase some crucial questions they hope interviewees will answer, such as: What were the beliefs and goals of the opposing sides in the war? What personal conflicts did you have? What was the most horrendous thing that happened to you? What did you learn from being part of this conflict? Ask students to take notes of the answers to each question. Follow up with a class discussion that compares and contrasts Tim's and the interviewee's ideas and experiences.

Summarizing the Book

PUTTING IT ALL TOGETHER

Use one or more of the following activities to help students summarize and review *My Brother Sam Is Dead.*

CLASS PROJECT: *Story Skits*

Assign groups of students to plan and act out the big incidents in the story chapters sequentially. For example, one group might act out Chapters 1 and 2, another group might act out Chapters 3, 4, and 5. Provide time for at least two story-sequence go-rounds. The first go-round should be put together fast and informally. Encourage the audience to talk about the high points of these first group skits, about what the actors revealed about the characters, and about how the skits might be improved. In the second go-round, actors can use audience comments and their own insights to improve their skits. When groups are satisfied with their dramatic renditions, they might tape record the drama or present it live to a larger school or family audience.

PARTNER PROJECT: *Sibling Stuff*

Partners can work together to identify the ways in which Tim and Sam bonded and worked together closely, and ways in which they differed and fought. Ask partners to make a visual to present their ideas. Partners might also consider and report on how they themselves agreed, disagreed, and reached resolutions as they carried out the project; how their insights about Tim and Sam apply to their relationships with their own siblings; what problems the Collier brothers (the co-authors of *My Brother Sam Is Dead*) may have encountered as they wrote the book.

INDIVIDUAL PROJECT: *Another Narrator*

After discussing what first-person point of view means, invite students to retell an incident in the book from another character's first-person viewpoint. Examples: tell about the fight in Chapter 6 from Betsy's first-person point of view; tell about Sam's disputes with his father from Sam's point of view; tell about the journey from Redding to Verplancks from the point of view of the horse, or of one of the cows in the cattle drive.

INDIVIDUAL PROJECT: *Art for the Story*

Ask students to imagine they've been asked to draw three big, full-color illustrations for a new edition of *My Brother Sam Is Dead*. The illustrations should show just three of the many exciting and important events in the story. Ask students to review the book, select and draw their illustrations, and write brief captions that tell what is happening.

EVALUATION IDEAS

Work with students to list a set of rubrics to use in assessing one of the summarizing projects. For example, a rubric for *Another Narrator* might include these objectives:

. Does the retelling stick to one character's point of view?

. Does the retelling show the main events?

. Does the retelling help readers know the narrator's feelings and thoughts?

. Does the retelling help us understand an incident in another way?

Possible Answers for Worksheets

page 14: . . . *loyal because:* We haven't suffered under English rule; we are citizens of England. . . . *fight for independence because:* England taxes us too much; we are a new nation and have the right to govern ourselves. . . . *avoid taking sides because:* We don't want to fight with our neighbors; we don't want our day-to-day lives interrupted.

page 15: Chapter 6: Ending: The message is intercepted and Tim is proved an unreliable messenger. Suspense: How will Tim face Mr. Heron? **Chapter 7:** Ending: Tim and his father reach Verplancks safely. Suspense: What will happen on the return trip? **Chapter 8:** Ending: Tim and his father have found a shelter. Suspense: How are they going to make it home? **Chapter 9:** Ending: Tim's father is gone and Tim goes home alone. Suspense: What's happened to Tim's father?

page 16: LATER (2) Tim begins to understand the colonial soldiers' point of view. (3) Tim sees that it's admirable to stand up for your opinions and ideals. (4) Tim learns that you can't avoid conflicts.

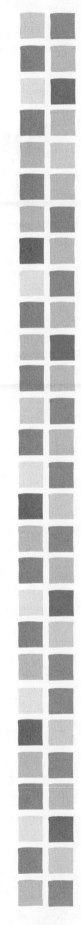

Name: _____

Conflicts

The citizens of Redding don't agree about how to handle the conflict between the British and the Colonists who want to be free of British rule. In the spaces, explain the three different opinions and include a quote from a character who shares that opinion.

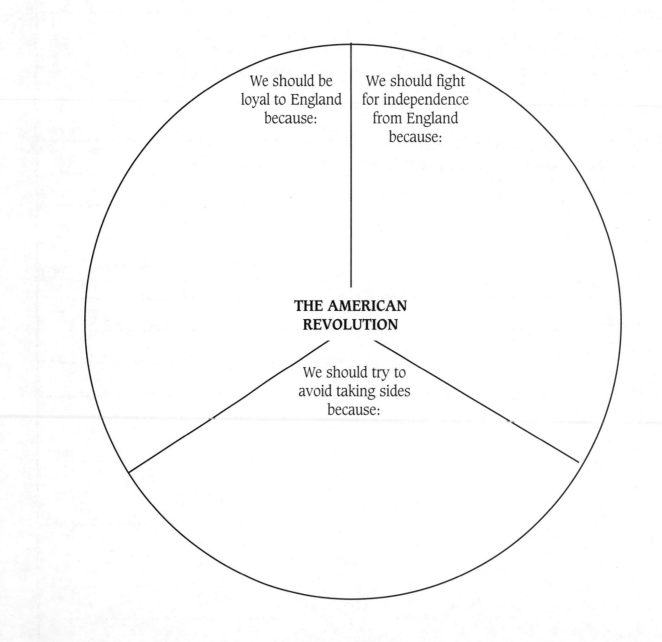

We should be loyal to England because:

We should fight for independence from England because:

THE AMERICAN REVOLUTION

We should try to avoid taking sides because:

Name: _____

Creating Suspense

Writers try to end chapters with incidents or ideas that make you want to know what happens in the next chapter! This is called *suspense*. Complete the chart by telling how the chapter ends and why you want to go on reading. An example is given to get you going.

CHAPTER	ENDS WITH	WHAT I WANT TO FIND OUT
3	Tim finding out that Sam is hiding nearby	Is Sam okay? Can Tim keep his father from knowing where Sam is?
6		
7		
8		
9		

Name: _____

Character Changes

Tim changes a lot during the war. The first column in the chart tells about Tim as the war begins. Complete the chart by telling about the changes in Tim's feelings and actions. An example is given to get you going.

AT FIRST	LATER
1. Tim worries and complains about how to do farm chores without Sam's help.	Tim finds out that he can do these tasks alone.
2. Tim completely agrees with his father about being loyal to England.	_____ _____ _____ _____
3. Tim thinks Sam is wrong to argue with their father.	_____ _____ _____ _____
4. Tim thinks that he and his family and neighbors are safe from the war.	_____ _____ _____